T0278181

Lapwing

First published 2024 by
Liverpool University Press
4 Cambridge Street
Liverpool
L69 7ZU

British Library Cataloguing-in-Publication data
A British Library CIP record is available

ISBN 978-1-80207-475-8 softback

Typeset by lexisbooks.com, Derby
Printed and bound in the USA by Integrated Books International

Lapwing

Hannah Copley

after Michael (otherwise known as)

Care has been given to maintain the anonymity of wounded and dead parties and, where possible, migrations, nesting and deaths have been fact-checked. Efforts have been made to account for translation error, deception and weather.

For anon after he was changed
And from his oghne kinde stranged,
A lappewincke mad he was,
And thus he hoppeth on the gras,
And on his hed ther stant upriht
A creste in tokne he was a kniht;
And yit unto this dai men seith,
A lappewincke hath lore his feith
And is the brid falseste of alle.

John Gower, 'Confessio Amanits'

Fabulous artificer, the hawklike man.
You flew. Whereto? Newhaven – Dieppe,
steerage passenger. Paris and back.
Lapwing. Icarus. Pater, ait.
Seabedabbled, fallen, weltering.
Lapwing you are. Lapwing he.

James Joyce, *Ulysses*

'Last seen in his winter plumage. Black and white
from a safe distance, metallic olive at close range.
Undertail coverts rufous, cinnamon tinged,
thin legs of bright red flesh. Almost raw looking.

Often mistaken for Hoopoe, which riles him.
Black pectoral band, white flank, with a dark ring
of colour beneath each eye the thickness of paint.
Longest feather of his crest once boasted at four inches.
Wings an iridescent green. Seen only when flying away.

Will go by Peewit, Plover, Tew-it, Lhapwynche,
Peet-Peet-Peet, Toppy, Kievit, Lappewincke, Pater,
Vanellus vanellus, Phillipeen.'

Is that all?

'Just that everything he says sounds like a question.'

Is that all?

And she remembers his stories.
        Lapwing, quenched,
slowly tumbling
 from high singularity
into the scrape of his thoughts.

        Thirst and craving
grounded into
a fuzzed eloquence,
panicked *pees weep weep*
softening into prose.

Here is something
to feather – this pull
skywards towards
a coded vagary,
        the willingness
to come down
from a high place
tied to a sliding scale
 of need.

Each morning,
the same boorish dogs,
the same dull threat
of obliteration,

her granted wildness
cordoned into
a neat rectangle.

She is done
with this wintering,
ready for the earth
to give, poised
to scratch for a more tender language.

I

Otherwise known as peewit, otherwise known
as tew-it, otherwise known as Vanellus vanellus
of the family Charadriidae, otherwise known as
plain old lappy nestling itself in the till, otherwise
known as diver found in its down in the centre
of some middle-of-nowhere, otherwise known as
wailer, otherwise known as waverer, as imp,
liar, as shrill green sky, as wader of the marsh,
slope, as flock, as Tereus turned and heckling
the cows, otherwise known as crown prince,
as crest, as sharp throat, as hare, otherwise known
as zigzag, soaring, dizzy, otherwise known as lost.

II

Otherwise known as green plover, controller
of seasons, shaman, crook, some skittish soul
turning everything it doesn't understand into a god:
god of the long grass, god of the cuckoo bird,
god of the gloved hand, god of the drought,
god of the estate, god of the sloping roof,
god of the silver tree, god of the frost,
god of the harvest, god of the metal roar,
god of the spinning white, god of the crop,
god of the unhatched, god of the death machine.

III

Otherwise known as nickname, posture,
as totter, raked ground. Lapwing, some sly
false flex, otherwise felt as a leap, as
tombstone shiver, as an ever-constant wince.

IV

Otherwise known as Peet-Peet-Peet. Plumage
primped and plucked to perfection, each bright
tail up like a rake, breast down, peck,
crown, otherwise known as hollow-man,
as bust-up, wing smacking the green fool that even
thinks to try his luck in these parts. Territory
as self-expression, otherwise known as belonging.
Peet-Peet-Peet. Otherwise known as showman,
as feathers, all dives and rolls and tumbles in time
to his spring song, swansong, his own pees-weep-
weep-weep. Otherwise known as seduction.

On waking

Hawk hovers
and falls from the firmament.

Peet, roosting in dawn frost,
thinks of mornings

spent enveloped
in the cotton womb

of her grandparent's bed.
Grief, she thinks,

is just an inflammation
of memory;

a fine tendon
slowly ripping itself

from wingtip
to beak.

On the difficulty of care

They once found him lulled beneath the concrete base
of the pylon, raggedy feather rucked
in leaf mould and mess. Smell of abandoned nest
caught in the grass. Green feather almost a pure dull.
Peet leaning in close enough to hear
his heart's violent thrum against the steady gust
of each commuter.

                    Lapwing, otherwise known
as Tew-it, remains where he tucks, body ringed
by the offerings of his brood: proffered crane fly,
larvae, a dozen wetland molluscs rotting
into a single organism. Slug bloated
and floating backwards in the waterlogged rut.

Indifference, otherwise justified as the quick nipping
of pain in the bud, pulls her to a safe distance.
Let the pylon loom, she thinks, let him kite himself
across this metal nation, let the A-road keep us
forever severed. A safe acreage between them.
Let him fashion his own flight home. Let him
disintegrate.

                    Love held
in leagues, love wrapped in steel and power cables,
love in concrete wings.

She thought it was just the regular carnage –

robin hurling its sweet tune from the copse,
the churlish red kites circling the field like clock hands,
crows fussing, as down below every straggler
and time waster and early bird and misdirected
and unhatched and already dead get threshed
to less than pieces –

but turns out there's to be a new crop. The old barley field
gets stripped of all memory. A brown field in March
bathed in sun and drilled fresh with sugar beet. Whistle is,
there are going to be shortages, or else surplus.

Of what, none of them know. All the old nests
wiped and sown and everyone ploughed back

into themselves. A new beginning on the old
burial ground. Already, the moles are moving in.

In which Peet repeats the lessons that Lapwing taught her

That a field is only a defined shape from above;

that the neatness of a field
on a piece of paper is a kind of shibboleth:
we are both wrong, it says. *We have never lived in this field.*

That a child will always
draw a square field;

that a field appears smooth to a drone
or a balloon or an airplane or a paraglider
or a sky lantern drifting slowly
downwards;

that a sky lantern
drifting towards the field portends death;

that a field is a series of jagged edges;

that a wheat field can be drawn as a racing
heartbeat;

that a wheat field can be drawn
as a disused needle factory;

that a wheat field can be drawn
as a hoard of spent arrows;

that a wheat field can be drawn as the sky's
scrubbing brush;

that each rutted valley is called ginnel;

that a field is part wrapper,

part coin, part buried screw, part crudely
painted stone;

that a field is only flat when seen from sky;

that a field roots itself
deeper than it is ever able to rise.

[SIGHTING

Newfoundland, November 1905

Handed in with a Turkey Buzzard. Not known to be travelling together. Found in excellent condition, being quite plump and its beautiful plumage scarcely ruffled. Collected about a mile inland from the seashore, making his way south, just outside the city limits. Almost impossible that he could have come direct across the Atlantic from his European home. Reporter is inclined to believe it may have been up somewhere in Greenland or Iceland, and been driven westward by the prevalence of strong gales of easterly and northeast winds.]

V

Birds have their demons too. Otherwise
heard as diversions. From the Latin to draw
or drag apart, Peewit has his ways of flitting,
of feigning each intended cry. Drink, violence,
no sense of direction, reneging on a promise
to mate for life, insolence. Otherwise known
as a deceit, for every short, sharp peet-peet-peet
there are ten tew-its that never catch the wind.
Here's one with a temper under his wing. Come
cat, he shrieks, come fox, come man with his
sharp tang and featherless glove, come cuckoo,
come endless sound, come parch, come hunger,
come pluck, come blunt serrated edge, come
raging monster blocking out the clouds.

VI

To be beleaguered, Peewit, otherwise known as
migrant, otherwise known as hoopoe, otherwise
known as flicker, must first settle into humdrum.
Winter hummock, scum trail twitching on the marsh,
the hare's breadth, exhaust cloud caught in an early
morning mist. The world keeps growing smaller.
Winnow, otherwise known as dart, otherwise caught
as a flash of white and black, pays his dues, scrapes
out the mud on a cold November Saturday, calls in
on neighbours, grubs, dozes belly-deep in the black
pond, crafts and recrafts his earlier misdeeds.

VII

Plain speech falling prey to full moons, myth
cresting through the ice. Dappled light, small
wonder. Tew-it, otherwise known as wandering
eye, displays the subtle, iridescent greens of his
carefully-preened plumage. This can work,
he reflects. Capricious order, domesticity as
an uneasy rest. As coagulant. Unearthly cries
drown out the common redshank, curlew,
each arrogant heron lording it on some nearby
log, the dull, incessant gossip of the coots:
chew-it, chew-it, chew-it.

VIII

One cloudless morning she let out a short, sharp
Peet, but otherwise they copulate in silence. Smell
of dirt, of warm feather, of dead worm, otherwise
known as aphrodisiacs. The way the light falls just so.
Lapwing, otherwise known as Tieve's Nacket,
as Toppyup, as winnowing wing, *ful of treacherye*.
But we all tell lies to get laid, says the lapwing chick.

Missing

Up late scavenging the reels
for a glimpse of him in someone else's story.
Image into video into image, eyes training
to the happiness of every other flock. Flick.

Peet, as is the custom, taking her comfort
in carefully distributed chaos.

Times Square. A child pelts into a blanket of pigeons,
arms flung wide into their grey skein. A singularity
scattered into two hundred sets of wings. Flick.

Grainy footage of a cockatoo bouncing
on a woman's head. Yellow crest unfurled, grey leg
ringed with its tiny metal chain. Flick.

A seagull rips the greater part of a Cornish pasty
out of a young man's hand. Flick.

Yet another clip of those fucking starlings. Flick.

Peet sees each one in the way that a tiny glass eye
sees, in the way that a wired open beak
sees. Flick.

Tring Museum. Two hundred
stuffed hummingbirds turn slowly
in a tombola of joy.

How endangered birds keep in touch

[Insert joke about pigeon post]

Lapwing, always so eloquent
over the phone, always wistful in letters.
Wish you were, scratches Lapwing
in his beautifully looping wing, *here*
in Missouri, Newfoundland, Kuwait.

Lapwing rendered perfectly in Arabic
on the back of a postcard from the UAE.
Please tell me what you've been doing,
requests Vanellus vanellus from Greenland.

Please find enclosed the short story about a mermaid that I
would like you to finish and send back to me. With no return
address and a passport full
of visa stamps.

Lapwing, otherwise homeless,
listening for Peet through
the radio silence. Peet, fatherless,
in receipt of paper.

In which Peet visits a doctor

'An endless craving
for wireworm and ground larvae;
a longing to press my face
full into the leaf mulch
and gorge; cramps.

I find myself flying backwards
into the stereotypes
I have learnt to abhor;
almost *lhapwynche*
in the uelthe of man,
almost liar, almost vessel
of something worth more.

And that False Flex,
otherwise known as plover,
otherwise known as filth dweller,
always bouncing
in and out of my thoughts.'

Two lines

Just a white plastic stick jutting
from the nest and a field gone over
to haunting – ghost marks, remains of a cross.

It says three minutes. Peet waits,
waits, with no wrist to check
so indeterminate time passes and the tiny wind turbine

reveals itself, floats to the surface of the sky pool.
Deep breath. Peet incubates anxiety, remembers
decapitated Eiderduck, the Canada goose

whipped open above her in the bright sun, robin
turned to snarge on the runway.
But it is a still day. It is a windless field.

It is only a crucifix of propellor.
It is so small and harmless.
Strange, and now life.

[SIGHTING

Canada, January 1927

At their first coming they appeared very weary, thin and
tame, but began at once to search for and find food on
the ground; and as they rested and gained strength, they
became wilder and noisier. No evidence is at hand as to
whether females as well as males were present, the small
differences between the sexes not being noticeable in the
circumstances. They soon crossed St. Lawrence Gulf to
Cape Breton and scattered over Nova Scotia, even finding
their way to the remote island of Grand Manan. In New
Brunswick they were quickly reported about the city of
St. John, where it is said that hundreds were soon killed
by a great snowfall.]

IX

Otherwise known as the king of tact. Circumlocution
tricks left in a trail of dark feathers. Recorded
by the peeping ornithologist as valiance. Otherwise
known as second nature. We can all dissemble. Life
and soul, one-man party, likes a drink, up for a laugh.
See, no fuss. Heard first as a weapon, lies more closely
resemble a bedtime story. A drawn-out cry for help.

X

Fear found as flush as a clutch of speckled light,
sown spring, enough for a basket, otherwise blown
clean crest, a cap for a babe. Some precious
quartet laid open for all the world and his friend,
for some Saxon notion of betrayal. Laid on the slake,
the comfortable scratch of dead grass. Decoy, snatch,
the endless cries of alarm. Swooping as redundant
motion, birth mistaken for a harvest.

XI

Otherwise known as failed utterance, how successful
can the lying hornpie really claim to be when faced
with the report: threatened, decline, in the red. Try
winnowing through those metaphors. Tew-it,
otherwise known as plover, known to his friends
as lappy, chooses not to bury his head in the sand,
but rather to drag his beak through the earth
in concentric circles to create a great hollow world.

XII

Otherwise known as lore unto himself.
Lapwing. Such intellect, such grace, such
promise, that killer voice – the kind of reedy
tenor tipsy birds can't help but fall for at a
house party, at picnics and evening jam sessions.
A clutch of partners, of habitats. Otherwise
known as a mosaic. Peet-Peet-Peet, otherwise
known as itchy feet, otherwise known as wind
change, as vagrant, as story keeper. Migration
offers endurance, novelty, otherwise known as
the hard-won maintenance of a myth, as survival.
Dissemblance as another breed of song.

Progress report

The water snail left to rot,

a sudden need for cow muck

and finally, this sharp pin prick of empathy.

What does it feel like to be stamped on?
What does it feel like to want joy and then receive it?
What does it feel like to be forever in motion?
What does it feel like to forget your child's name?

What do I know
of the brood before me –

a whole life lived and pecked to fluff –

except for the carnage that sodden
love can leave in its wake.

Each daily observation,
each survey with a view to save him,
the endless dreaming of his outline

      concludes fatherhood
to be a temporary resurrection

a wetland given leave from its draining.

I am so lost in all those years of dissembling,
every memory dis-assembled

that it's possible that I'm hovering above nothing.

I know it's possible
that I can never be done.
I know it's possible that I never really met him.

Mnemonic technique

How to mourn   something
never known   as anything: one single
fragment of egg shard
gently tucked into the damp mud
beneath the nest   daily thinning to dust.

One last impression
of what once split   a heart

imprinted in a finely painted
blood map. Life forever unlocated

on the shell.

    I would imbue that blood trail if I could take it all back
but how to re-trace hops, how to pretend to embrace stillness
as if it could adjust the outcome; clip my own wings.

Here

in the church of the heart
lost objects abound. Here in the church
of the heart

                I am the tallest thing for miles.

Miscellaneous wants

WANTED, HORSE,
Cob size, for small place, to cart
and plough. – State price. – Apply.

WANTED, LAPWING EGGS,
highest prices given. – Apply.

WANTED, LAPWING EGGS,
until 14th April. Prices high. – Apply.

WANTED, LAPWING EGGS,
as in former years. Highest price given. – Apply.

I will buy LAPWING EGGS,
from now until 14th April. High prices. – Apply.

WANTED, CHILD,
to bring up. – Apply.

[SIGHTING

Shemya, Alaska, 2006

Loitering near the military base in October. Flushed at
sixty metres. As he became airborne uttered a sharp call.
Pigeon-like size, dark plumage, large paddle-shaped wings,
and crest identified him unmistakably. Last seen circling
a bar in Northern Europe, last seen nesting in Mongolia.
Flew two-hundred metres to the west and landed in deep
beach grasses adjacent to a sewage-treatment pond. Stalked
and collected (52° 43' N, 174° 07' E). Archived as a study
skin and partial skeleton with two frozen genetic samples.]

XIII

Known first as prodigal, cracked shell, survivor
of drought, summer son, otherwise held up
as miracle, as proof of the decoy nest. First
felt as Cristātus, sole endured, first and only
to leave, as bare-crowned, damp crest, as not-
yet devoid of all faith. There could be no witnesses
to marvel. Gratitude told as a readiness to flee.
Each writhing meal, the wet-nosed dog, the circling
hawk. Cramped conditions breed contempt, the cruel
weight of sibling love. Expectation, like a cuckoo
taking shelter in the crudely scratched out nest.

XIV

Hymn for seasons. Hymn for every frame.
Hymn for births, deaths, and migrations.
Hymn for each mislaid babe, smashed egg,
snatched chick, wing trodden and crumbled
underfoot. Hymn for the cold. Hymn for
the gone. Hymn for every imagined ghost.
Hymn to ward off approaching catastrophe.
Hymn to know it. Hymn to acknowledge an
over-eagerness to feel besieged. Hymn
to recognise threat. Hymn to stay still
long enough to see it approach.

XV

Lapwing resents the accusation that never having
to exhaust every problem, every possibility, never
having to stay, means never having to discover
the hard meaning of care, of love not as a feeling,
but as a labour. There is labour enough, labelled
as necessity, labelled chance, in simply staying alive.

XVI

Brother, cousin, uncle, mate. Otherwise known
as excess baggage, as dying weight. Stillness as
a series of parries, otherwise known as the long
meaning of eschew; the same pronouncements
repenting of themselves over many years. Stillness
felt as forgetting what it means to be anything
but quarry, as collateral loss. Plucked up and restless,
Hoopoe and the gang make tracks, head south,
attend to their needs, loop back. Love as contraband,
flight as freedom smuggled over invisible thread.
There is no stopping them. Otherwise heard as no one.

Family tree

One cousin exploded
while breaking on the Falkland Islands;

another settled in Pennsylvania,
one more to Vancouver.
Lovely part of the world to lay a clutch;

twenty-five close relations
hammered to death in a storm
somewhere between Dover and Bhutan;

twelve starved near Morecambe;

two ancient friends in Southern France;

seven shorn to straw in Norfolk;

forty-nine eggs picked off
in two hours from Friesland;

seven shot in Newfoundland;

one son, mislaid;

the entire brood
eaten in Hertfordshire;

one ex-girlfriend roosting
somewhere in Kent.

Black and white

A typical evening for the remainers –
just the regular October light show
from the B-Road.

Here comes
the inevitable drag. All the same tricks.
All the regular haunts. Peet, sitting atop
the empty nest, begins her costume brainstorm:

1. Halloween as a spray of gravel;
2. Halloween as a scattered pack of clubs;
3. Halloween as a chess board and all
its pieces chucked up into a hurricane;
4. Halloween as a terrible explosion
in the domino factory;
5. Halloween as spoondrift in the dark.

All group costumes, she reflects.
All requiring the flock and their inevitable
ups and downs.

Peet remembers her chickhood
of satsuma rind, her squash threaded with twine.
Almost flying.

All those black evenings
watching *Kes*, face behind the cushion,
light left on in the hall.

In which bears eat her

There she goes dreaming of a place un-held by gravity,
dreaming of a four-day week and the four-week course
in fashion management that she saw advertised on the side

of the moving machine, dreaming of bears that will eat you alive,
dreaming of moving around various stocks and shares
and consolidating all the pension pots into one manageable

and easily trackable account. The starlings are everywhere
and she's longing to sleep and not be so alive in her body,
to not be on the verge of busting out of her own feathers

in frustration. What is all this fuss, she thinks. From what
continent does anger migrate? Where does it summer?
Peet grinds her beak against the day's particular whetstone.

The burst water pipe spills its flood

Edges ever closer, and still nothing.
Peet, second offspring, midnight
insomniac, panic tweeter, dissembler, squirms
within the confines of the dirty nest.

Lapwing, otherwise known as missing,
last heard on a deleted voicemail from ten years ago,
last heard the night before at the thirty-seven
minute mark of the birdsong ASMR. His questioning
second note waking her from light sleep.

He's still working then.

A nerve tingle, an electric jolt
of recognition before nothingness settles
back into the narrow band of nerve around her skull.

       Voice of Lapwing, fading
into barn owl, fading
into blackbird, fading into robin, fading
into advert, fading
into acrylic fingernails tapping
against a dry bar of soap, fading
into a wet mouth wordlessly opening and closing, fading
into an endless cave of white noise.

[SIGHTING

Glasgow, 1833

On the 6th April last, Philp, the complainer, who resides
with his father at Gallatown, and is now only fifteen years
of age, had occasion to go to the house of an individual
in the immediate vicinity; and on his return home, about
three o'clock in the afternoon, be met with two other boys,
one not exceeding twelve years of age, and the other sixteen,
accompanied by two mongrel dogs. Whilst standing with
these boys on the public road, the attention of Philp
and his companions was suddenly attracted by the cry
of a "peeseweep" or lapwing, whose motions seemed to
indicate that her nest could not be distant; and impelled,
as is alleged, by a feeling natural to boy of their age, they
all entered the field where they had noticed the lapwing,
in the hope of discovering her nest. But they had scarcely
done so when they observed Lord Loughborough, son of
the Earl of Roselyn, who was at that time at Dysart House,
the residence of his father, riding furiously towards them.
Alarmed at the unexpected apparition of the noble game
preserver, the poor boys, in order to avoid being ridden
down by him, endeavoured to get out of the field, and
two of the three appear to have succeeded in doing so.
But Philp, it would seem, was less fortunate; for being
overtaken by Lord Loughborough, he was ridden down
by the gallant horseman and, not content with this, his
Lordship is alleged to have then dismounted, and beaten
the boy severely.]

XVII

Nothing muscular enough. Nothing
wholly anarchic. Lapwing simply wishes
violence upon the whole of Birdworld.
Upon the whole of himself. See, nothing
radical. Merely a starling prejudice. Hatred
tightening the beak, self-loathing expressed
as a series of bird calls across the empty
dual carriageway. Lapwing, crying to go
backwards, crying to undo, tapping his foot
to the soil to draw out the worm,
crying a gentle and vaguely catchy tune.

XVIII

Consolation's pop gun hits its mark not once
but for the round. Lapwing, otherwise known as
Kievit, otherwise known as punter, is left in reverie.
Wing propped, half-cut through with grief,
pee-wit senses the moment to spill forth
his history of time, otherwise known as
the philosophy of imprecision: that old array
of hours stuck out to frost, of all the dead days
caught between the sun and his uncovered eyes.
The clock ticks, Lapwing has his notched bone,
his moon, names himself as his own time reckoner.
Circle of stone, auspicious weed, wireworms
grubbing in a perfect line beneath the rock –
all ways of catching up to death. Tew-it, otherwise
answering to Dix-huit, prefers the clean erasure
of the calendar, time's geometry shorn through
and left to dry in the field's squared plot. The field
in its scythed flatness giving all parts of time
an equal weight. Here is a place to be the tallest thing
for miles. Here is a spot to wait to dissolve.

XIX

But what number dream song is this?
What other name has ever been accepted
beyond the given? Why change now.
What else to do but lap-lap-lap at himself
when he thinks nobody is watching. Lapwing
considers applying for keystone status
but without the paperwork
or proof of worth or impact beyond grief's
extended vector, beyond spirit and its acrid tinge
what is there to write. Every feeling like this
is a small extinction; a briefly airborne narrative
left to bleed into a furrow.

In which we can reinvent everything about ourselves in response

Fecklessness as a life pursuit,
      migration
as the sole antibody of solitude:

      easy to choose instead
to be anodyne, to choose to apprehend
only those things that remain mud bound,

to choose the role of stenographer
of a father's throat.
    Perhaps,
this is the flight path
      into my own bitterness,

      or rather away from it –
mapping each shadow
    to remedy
    walking through it.

Perhaps
    all this is nothing –

wild goose chase, vanity

some slow ebb
    of a lifetime's worth of
unspent petulance.

        There is no looking backwards when flying. It is
        only from a point of stillness that the rotation
        can begin.

All this searching
a long defence
of my own discomfort.

Which rotation?

She remembers the feeling,
so peculiar, of her body

eating itself. The cage
where she sits in her own ragged

covert waiting to be set loose,
the broken *Pees-weep-weeps*

of the crowded reserve.
Curtained against their indignity,

she still heard every last peewit,

every sorry tew-it, each sodden
lappy dressed in his sadness,

all the old gang. Here's
where they'd been hiding.

[SIGHTING

Thames foreshore, 2019

Sighted up to the bronze vents in muck, a whole group of
them larking without a permit along the foreshore close
to the Tower. Visibly drunk, underparts caked, one was
seen swaying in receipt of a sovereign penny, one bent
aglet and a thin piece of pottery the same colour as its
breast. May have been a feather. When approached, every
member of the party rose approximately twenty feet into
the air and began a series of steady pee-wits. When asked
to descend, suspects instead fired a set of clay squidges
towards the vicinity of the first response team and then
absconded up-river.]

XX

With numbers in such sharp decline, with the state of
agriculture as it is, with the increased conversion of
arable land to pasture, with the use of increasingly
large machinery, with the sale of land to developers,
with the melting of the ice caps, with rising sea levels,
with habitat destruction, with weather phenomenon,
with the drainage of wet grassland and the continued
poaching of eggs for the seasonal menus of expensive
restaurants, with the hot weather leading to the early
cutting of grass for silage rather than hay, with the
resurgence of *Brideshead Revisited* reenactors, with
the gradual but irrevocable estrangement from those
formally known as his flock, tew-it is forced to think
about legacy. Having no solicitor, tew-it, otherwise
known as peet-peet-peet, otherwise known as Vanellus
vanellus of the family Charadriidae, acts as his own
executor, draws up his estate: twig, feather, fluff, dried shit,
corn husk, dried grass, clod, some calcified, some not. Tew-it,
otherwise known as Lapwing, otherwise known as progenitor,
cries out the names of his surviving issue: Peet-Peet-Peet.

XXI

Never egret, never owl, never hawk or crow,
never able to feel himself, never man, never allowed,
maintained even now as myth, as a moving coordinate,
as target, kept as a creature, observed and pitied
from an uncrossable distance.

XXII

Some plastic tag, some earmarked ground, some
ready-scraped nest. Lapwing's young reserve
his gilded cage in twitcher's paradise. Lawn pet.
Protection order, otherwise known as clipped wing,
otherwise known as death knell.

XXIII

When is the moment to admit
to this history? To shake off
the small, unasked for pretence
and unburden my body of feathers. This is
a tribute in the same way that a stuffing is a tribute,
in the same way that a bell jar and some moss
is a forever home. We are already in the back room
and I am searching through the cabinet for
the right glass eyes to let him see my great achievement.

And you can't say he didn't. Lapwing, landing fifteen minutes past the hour and fifteen minutes into the meeting, crest hackled. Here to join the chapter. Here to strut the steps. Tew-it, hater of the crow's happiness, hater of the morose coot, hater of all skylark depression, hater of goose fat, hater of the way they celebrate each other, hater of their books, hater of the way they hug and clasp each other's wings, hater of the coffee, hater of cheap snacks, hater of his image in their black eyes.

[SIGHTING

Poland, 2011

July 2011 in the Jeziorsko dam reservoir. Spotted walking slowly through the transect of mudflat designated for sampling. No paralysis of the neck, no obvious lethargy. Thought not to be afflicted. When dissected, spleen, liver, kidneys and digestive tract were found not to contain traces of type C botulinum toxin. Stomach empty of larvae. No signs of intoxication.

See graph 2a (with positive reading from four common coots and two mallards for comparison).]

XXIV

Belly risen; lung full; the never-ceasing shake.
Lapwing, heart sore. Just a small bird, otherwise known
as homesick boy, as a broken body settling
into a strange field.

XXV

Litany, otherwise known as requiem, otherwise
known as send off. The last of a dying breed,
up for laugh, king of the preeners, iridescent in
his own light, the mourners peck, as they flutter up
and down on a great, invisible trampoline. Loved
in absentia, lore abounds in the hairline cracks of wings.
Father, bounder, besieged. Euphemisms fall around
like feathers. Lapwing, otherwise heard as panic,
otherwise heard as parry, otherwise heard as parent,
otherwise never seen, shakes off each well-meaning
predator, lays low in a neighbouring field. Time
to get clean, time to disappear, time to prepare
for his re-admittance to the party.

Lettings

Still,
     a bird never talked
about as a painful thing
to happen

to everyone
   who loved him.

All this can be understood
as a long prospecting of all that
     rich, unspoilt common ground;
                              as a
dispassionate enquiry into
the death of flight;

as a survey of the silhouettes
of birds;

as a sonic record of a spot
in the sky.

No lesson but that love
is not a wishbone
     but a shredder.

Nothing to do but lie
in the fresh dirt

and hear the lorries
and watch paper

revenants
   swooping

nowhere
in particular.

[I'm almost sure that Daedalus merely wished to show his son that no border could hold him, that high enough, the skyline would remain constant, that journeying is myriad. [I'm] almost sure that Daedalus merely wished to show his son what porosity could feel like.]

Tribute

There goes the wind and nowhere
to shelter, hedgerow a mere myth.
Peet, the last bird in this flattened world,
makes her way towards the temple
called Lonely Oak, picks between the shrine
of brightly painted stones. Peet,
pinned in an endless lunar turntable.

The field has no border and the crucible turbine
is always so unsure of its delineation.
Each speckled egg, she visualizes, is a trinket
dangling from a blue thread; each lung
a thumbprint of cloud in the darkening sky.

I am always about to lose my way.
And in the distance, Lapwing. In the near distance,
Lapwing. Nearest, Lapwing. Same old,
same old, life as thin as contact paper.

[SIGHTING

Cambridge, 2021

Eyes glassy in Fitzwilliam Street, standing at his full height between a swan and a European woodpecker. Lapwing, inserted into a family tableau, mounted as the loving father of three dead chicks. Feathers stiff, neck stuffed into a position of high alert, Lapwing, quiet star of the Birds of the British Isles, stares outwards past the fluffed bodies of his brood towards the diorama of sea bird habitats.]

XXVI

Otherwise known as no reply. As silent heron,
silent hookwink, silent coot. A clear Peet-Peet
shrilled alone in a fallow field, otherwise known
as devoid. Knowledge felt as drained pond,
louring sky, slaked grass, flushed clutch, as
otherworld. Lapwing, transmuted, remains
unmoved. Vision begets sound begets touch
begets flight. Tew-it nestled in comfortable
obscurity. Hoopoe culled. Pees-wit shorn open
with the yellow crop. Knowledge as throat, as
beak, as orange foot, as sheen. Knowledge as
exacting science, as lapwing, otherwise known
as lapwing, otherwise known as lapwing, otherwise
known as lapwing, otherwise known as nothing.

Copyright of the author

[This feather. Click. That regurgitated leatherjacket. Click. Mollusc remnant, an unhatched egg snatched up from the nest and rolled into a handkerchief like a piece of pie. Click. Lemonade then urine in a coke bottle. Careful. A Mahler symphony playing on a loop beneath the nest. Nothing discernible. At five we take down the radio and the tiny lens, remove the headset and the speakers and walk back to the van.]

Acknowledgements

Thank you to the editors of *POETRY*, *Poetry & Audience* and *Blackbox Manifold* for publishing earlier versions of some of the poems in *Lapwing*.

For creative advice, support, encouragement, inspiration, birdsong recordings, coffees and childcare, thanks at various points and in different ways to Jon Glover, John Whale, Helen Mort, Emma Trott, Matthew Morrison, Monica Germanà, Guy Osborn, Michael Nath, the Westminster creative writing students, Claire Protherough, Aaron Kent, Kim Bridger, Leila White, Sophie Morley, Courtney Thornalley, Louise Parrott, Golnoosh Nour, Matthew Bates and Dana Niamh.

Endless gratitude to Claire Pelly, whose careful reading and friendship made *Lapwing* possible, and to all the Gales for putting up with us.

Thanks and admiration to Deryn Rees-Jones for her belief and support, her editorial insight and her gentle encouragement to push further and sit with discomfort. It made everything better.

To my family, and to all those who loved and cared for my father, my love and gratitude.

To my husband, Nick, and my mother, Fiona, I owe so much. For Emmeline and Kit, a glimpse.

For support with alcohol addiction alcoholchange.org.uk

For those trying to support someone living with alcoholism al-anonuk.org.uk

bloated appendix

of Lapwing. Wrapped tight in his dark vestment,

barely thawed, the bird hops in amongst the genetic material,
touches his beak to a label for *Maize*.

Tremble equates to flutter equates to a shrill catch
of air against the beak. Svalbard sounds like a train

scratching its track, like wind screwing its way
through a loose rivet. Barely a feather, barely a curled

foot left of him and still throwing his voice down
the converted mine shaft. *Peet* bouncing off the insulation,

heard as a broken bell through the farthest corridor
of the store. Doorways to nowhere, and the cold

finding its way into every cranny of dying cell.

This must be the fourth week of wordlessness. Stow away, maker
of tiny peck marks on twenty-nine seed containers,

unwarranted accession, peeler of the faint church bell,
tracer of tectonic death, Vanellus vanellus

pays his tribute to the canary bird and the polar bear
corpse. Today's task, the Brassica shelf, followed by a final

decision on where to nest in this deterrent world.